Patrick Rodgers

Head in Hands
(Stories and songs)

Patrick Rodgers

DEDICATION

I dedicate this to the two women that have made me the man I am today. First and foremost, my Mom, Josephine Rodgers. You set an example of what a strong parent should be. Your strength showed me how to be the father I have become. Secondly, my daughter, Allicia Rodgers. You have taught me so many lessons, you inspire me every day and you are my reason for living. I couldn't love someone any more than I love you.

CONTENTS

Discography

The Bootleg Ep – 2003
…But It's A Good Suck – 2003
It Is What It Is – 2008
The Circle Tapes – 2009
The Party's Over - 2011

To all the people I've had the privilege of playing music with…

Frank Boss
Tom Glovan
Josh Sare
Jamie Viera
Jen Clayton
Paul Butler
Karl Haeussel
Ed Hart (my only teacher)
Ben Jordan
Mike Jones
Billiam
Jay
Basil
Alex
Satan's Flapjacks
Julie's Left Nipple
Allstar Posse
Drunk Hippies on Probation
Housebroken
M-16's
Citizen Seeks Revenge
Springfield Cubs
Ship High In Transit
Victims of Circumstance
Ya'll
52 Cards Short

And so many more….

GET IN YOUR CAR

Get in Your Car was the first "song" I had ever written. I wrote the basic guitar riff while toiling away in Tiki Village, a shitty trailer park in Largo, Florida, back in 1996-1997. I would often come home from working at an auto repair shop and strum my guitar while drinking copious amounts of beer. The riff was simple enough for a new guitar player and it sounded halfway decent. The chorus was solidified while practicing at Circle Studios. A good friend of the band, Frank Haiduk, walked into our practice one day while we were in the middle of playing the song, which at the time was an instrumental. During the "chorus" part, he grabbed a mic and began singing "Get in your car, Drive it real far". When I finally understood what he was saying, I quickly wrote the rest of the lyrics to the song. The song, like many that I wrote, revolves around a relationship I while young and often drunk. A girl I had broken up with called me one night and tried to convince me that she was pregnant and it was imperative that we back together. She never liked my friends and gave me the "it's time to settle down" speech. I knew she was lying, and after she took a test, it was clear to see it was just a ploy to get back into my life. At the time, I was strictly in a "Bro before Hoe" mentality. I know that's not PC, but it's the truth.

Get in Your Car

Should have seen her face when I said go away
 I don't want you hanging round here
Must have been misled by all the sex we had
But hey I drank a lot of beer
Should have said she wanted someone to be with
From now and through eternity
I am not that man she wants to grow old with
I have a yearning to be free

Can't you see, I'm never be the man that you want me to be
Don't you be, so bothersome and irate, you should just move on

Get in your car, drive it real far
I'm not the guy that you want me to be
Although things have changed, I'll always remain the same
Loyal to my friends and all my family

She called me up, about a quarter to five
She said she got knocked up, and the kid it was mine
I know it's a lie, I always strap when I play
You see it's just this girl's way to try and make me stay

Can't you see, I'll never be the man that you want me to be
Don't you be, so bothersome and irate, you should just move on

Get in your car, drive it real far
I'm not the guy that you want me to be
Although things have changed, I'll always remain the same
Loyal to my friends and all my family

I'm not the bitch that you want to see

Get in your car, drive it real far
I'm not the guy that you want me to be
Although things have changed, I'll always remain the same
Loyal to my friends and all my family

Get in your car (3X)

NINE BUCKS AN HOUR

Nine Bucks an Hour was another song written half drunk at Tiki Village. As with most of the songs, I had a basic riff at first, then added lyrics. I started thinking about a girl I had dated. At the time, we were both straight edge in high school, no drinking or drugs. I graduated a year before her. I turned down a full scholarship to a college in Georgia to keep our relationship going, I figured I'd just wait till she finished high school, then try and get into a college near wherever she went. I know, not the smartest decision. During her Senior year, she wanted to start partying and began hanging out with many of the pot/pill heads in the area, many of which I knew from the neighborhood. It didn't last, obviously.

I also pulled inspiration from a friend that spent most of his time locked up in his home, smoking pot and masturbating. He was that guy we all knew that had no plan for his future, but you've been boys since way back so you keep hanging out with them. He took advantage of most of our mutual friends, often steeling money or using their name to run up utility bills and such.

I mashed these two personalities together and wrote this song. Mainly it centers on how people change and there is really nothing you can do to stop it from happening. Sometimes you just must walk away.

Nine Bucks an Hour

I saw you just the other day, you were contemplating
What to do with all your life
Spending most of it at home, quietly masturbating
Over pictures of girls that won't give you the time
Should have asked you what was up, how have things been going?
But your eyes were sunken in your skull
With your blank stare and those needle tracks I know you'll never
Get to know what life's about

I just don't believe, the things that you say, the words that you bleed
And I know that I, just can't stand to sit and watch you die
Oh yeah yeah yeah

I've known you since the seventh grade, then we went to college
You got fucked up with the wrong crowd.
Started shooting up and stealing from the ones that counted
And now you're dying by yourself

I just don't believe, the things that you say, the words that you bleed
And I know that I, just can't stand to sit and watch you die
Oh yeah yeah yeah

You told me things would never be the same
You're gone and I think I'm the one to blame
I thought our love was never ending
But it's your lies I've been defending
I tried to hug you hold you every night
You'd lie and try to start a big ass fight
Your cheating left me here a broken man
But now I'm rocking in the Allstar Band
Oh, oh oh, Nine Bucks an hour baby gotta go(X2)

I just don't believe, the things that you say, the words that you bleed
And I know that I, just can't stand to sit and watch you die
Oh yeah yeah yeah

SMOKIN' STONES

Smokin' Stones was a fun track to write. At the time, I was living in a hotel suite. Not a good hotel, but I had a living room, kitchen, bedroom, and bathroom, cable and phone, so it was comfortable. I had invited my bassist at the time, Frank Boss, over to write some songs. I told him I had been working on a new one, but that was bullshit. I just wanted a drinking buddy that evening. After work, we met up and he pulled out his bass. I just started playing a riff, making it up as I went along. The chord progression was simple, but it sounded cool. Frank asked what the next part was. I had no idea. I just grabbed a D chord, started playing, and it worked. Frank thought it was an awesome track and we ran with it. It felt amazing to be able to write such a fun song in so little time. That pushed me to write more and more. I kept trying to relive that moment and feeling through the years, most of the time I failed, but every so often, I'd strike gold.

The lyrics tell the story of someone dealing with depression and self-doubt. It may be semi-autobiographical. Although living in a hotel was cool, I was living in a hotel. I had no idea how to fix my life and was just trying to find my place in the world. I was heavily into drugs at the time, often partying till 3 or 4 in the morning, just to stumble into work at 7. It was a vicious cycle that took its toll on me. I think this song helped me realize what I was doing and I helped me to start making the changes that I needed to make.

SMOKIN' STONES

I see your life, why's it so complicated
You spend your time, Broke down and so frustrated
Suffocated by the city smog
It's hard to concentrate when your mind's distraught

Sit back, Relax
You live your life to damn fast
Sit Back, Relax
You like to think you're all that
Sit back, Relax
Some say you might be on crack
I guess you're always smokin' stones

You heard the lies, but still you sit and listen
You lack the time, mind, strength, faith and conviction
Never moving forward and you've lost all sense of time
The lies you tell, the things you steal. You're no friend of mine

Sit back, Relax
You live your life to damn fast
Sit Back, Relax
You like to think you're all that
Sit back, Relax
Some say you might be on crack
I guess you're always smokin' stones

I see your life, why's it so complicated
You spend your time, Broke down and so frustrated
You heard the lies, but still you sit and listen
You lack the time, mind, strength, faith and conviction

SEX OR POLITICS

Sex or Politics is an interesting song. I had the lyrics floating around in my head for a long time. I was jamming in my living room one Sunday morning when I played a chord progression I never tried before. I don't know the names of the chords in the progression but they sounded good together and the lyrics just kind of fit. Keep in mind that I've never had a guitar lesson in my life. The lyrics are ambiguous, they could relate to either the political environment we live in or the relationships we go through in our everyday life. The lyrics came to me while I was at work, I wrote them on scrap pieces of paper I had in my work area throughout the day, which is how many of my songs were written. I often put all my heart and soul into my lyrics, as basic as they may be, but they are my inner thoughts and feelings at that specific time. At the time I wrote this, we were in an election year, and I was going through another break-up, which seems to be the only time I can write. This song represents how close one's thoughts on sex or politics may be.

SEX OR POLITICS

Please explain to me how this could all be real
I've seen it many times before and it seems to have that mass appeal
You know I've studied all your pages
And I've read between your lies
Hidden in your cryptic messages, the blueprint of our demise

If you really knew me, you would know that I am real
So stop wasting all my…. Time
Consequences move me, I know what's the deal
You take what's yours, I'll keep what's mine

Words I told to you were only said in jest
Far be it for me to assume I'm so much better than the rest
You know I've
Listened to the stories you told while you were on your back
Can you even tell the difference from what's fiction? And what is fact?

If you really knew me, you would know that I am real
So stop wasting all my…. Time
Consequences move me, I know what's the deal
You take what's yours, I'll keep what's mine

Can you hear it? It's coming!
I've seen right through your lies look me straight in the eyes!
Can you feel it? It's coming!
Footsteps on the street the sound of your demise.

If you really knew me, you would know that I am real
So stop wasting all my…. Time
Consequences move me, I know what's the deal
You take what's yours, I'll keep what's mine

MANTITS

Mantits was a hard song to write. It was originally called "Sappy Break-up Song", but I felt like I grew a pair of man-tits whenever I sang it. I wrote the lyrics while married. I always knew the relationship wouldn't last, but I had always hoped that it would. I met my wife in high school and fell in love with her instantly. I always knew I would marry her. I always felt like we were meant to be together. There was something about her that I couldn't stop thinking about…for YEARS. It had nothing to do with her looks, it was the way her eyes locked with mine, the way it felt like our souls were interlocked. She was the inhale to my exhale.

We never dated in school, in fact, I only reconnected with her 16 years later. It felt like serendipity. The connection was irrefutable, but the timing was wrong. Unfortunately, by the time I had reconnected with her, she was in a different place. I don't regret my time with her, it was honestly some of the only times I have ever been able to be myself. Unfortunately, she was looking for more than I had to offer. She will always be the love of my life. We recorded this song once, the day she told me she wanted a divorce. It was a strange coincidence. We had the recording session planned for weeks in advance, she dropped the bomb on me right before I walked out the door. It was a long ride to the studio. When I was singing the lyrics, they obviously felt extra heavy. You can hear it in my voice, the anger, sadness, confusion, and frustration.

MANTITS

Take the time to get to know me, 'Cause I'm sinking slowly, into your arms
You know that every word that I told you, and every little thing I showed you
Never meant to cause you harm
Got your bags all packed sitting here, by the front door
"Please don't go away" you said, "I can't stay here no more"

And I would do anything to make it be the way it used to be
Oh why can't you see? I need you here with me.

(CHORUS)
But you're moving on. And I don't know what's going on.
How you could walk away from this life.
But you're moving on.
I don't know if I'll be strong, and I, know that I can't survive,
Without you in my life.

Days are slowly creeping by, and I don't know why;
I start to cry when I think of you
The memory of our first kiss. The way we talked about having kids.
Wish there was something that I could do.
I tried to make us work. You said I suck and I'm such a jerk.
But to you I never lied.

And I would do anything to make it be the way it used to be
Oh why can't you see? I need you here with me.

(CHORUS)

I see you out with him. You flash a smile I fake a grin
Hiding pain that I feel inside
I see you out with him, it makes me want to commit a sin
But I know that isn't right

(CHORUS)

SHAME ON ME (HARRY'S SONG)

I always had this song in my head, since I was a little kid. It was never really composed and the lyrics often changed, but I always knew I wanted to write a song to my father. I wanted to have him hear it and feel bad for leaving me and my younger brother all alone. I must have been 5 or 6 when he left our lives. When my mother, younger brother and I returned home to Massachusetts from a "vacation" in Florida, we stayed in a hotel, then we loaded into his van and he dropped us off in New Hampshire.

I saw him a couple times shortly after he split from my Mom. I remember once when he showed up around Easter time I greeted him at the door with my hockey stick, not to play, but I wanted to beat him with it. He eventually stopped coming by to pick my brother and I up. I never understood what happened. He was just gone. I spent many of my adolescent years lying to my friends about him. I would say he traveled for work, I would make up stories of fun times we spent together. I was the only boy in boy scouts that didn't have a father to participate in the Father-son activities.

About 6 or 7 years later, he showed up again. We spent a week or two together, but he mainly dropped me off with other relatives while I was there. We never really got to have any conversations. That was the last time I saw him. I wrote him a letter after high school, wanting to connect on some level. I wanted a father. I got two letters in response, both with different hand writing and tone. It was clear someone else had written one of the letters pretending to be him. I replied, but never heard from him again. I've heard he thought I was wanting money from him, but all I wanted was a dad. I tried to locate him again after my daughter was born, I wanted her to have the family I never had. When searching for his name online I came across his obituary. Hell of a way to find out your father is dead. I still have the picture he sent me of himself. I often wonder what life would have been like with him in it. From what I hear he was an amazing person to be around, just not a good dad.

SHAME ON ME (HARRY'S SONG)

Hello,
It's been a while since I've seen you last
A lot has changed, a lot of time has passed
At least we made it here
I learned to drive from a drunk named Ed
An old dirt road and a beat up Chevette
I know I drank a beer that summer night
I got a kid and a minivan that's blue
I've been arrested maybe a time or two
Crazy how those years they fly by so fast
You could have called or maybe dropped me a note
I don't remember the last time we spoke
Oh lord no…Shame on me!

Shame on me, Shame on me, Oh lord no…Shame on me. (2X)

All those nights I sat up in bed
So many thought swirling in my head
What did I do that was so fucking wrong?
Felt like I was drowning in a sinking boat
No sense of safety, no signs of hope
I had to learn to swim all on my own
Mom tried real hard she did the best she could do
I often wondered, where the hell are you?
Screaming angry words into a paneled wall
You could have called or maybe dropped me a note
I don't remember the last time we spoke
Oh lord no…Shame on me!

Shame on me, Shame on me, Oh lord no…Shame on me. (2X)

P.W.T.

P.W.T – Another song I wrote after the end of a toxic relationship. It's self explanatory. Obviously, I use song writing to deal with relationship issues.

P.W.T

I know you've got something
Up your sleeve
The way your eyes their looking
Right through me
Lately, you've been wandering
All over town
Sliding those thighs wide open
If they lay money down

And I see….
That you….
Could never be…
Will never be…. YEAH!

Your whispers are so soothing
In my ears
The game you play is confusing
Let me tell you dear
People, they're all talking
Behind your back
They say, she's so damn beautiful
For pure white trash

And I see….
That you….
Could never be…
Will never be…. YEAH!

COOLER

Cooler was a song that I wrote while working at Dependable Driveshaft in Pinellas County Florida. This is one of those songs I wrote while possibly under the influence of various substances. I was thinking that others feel the same about the things hanging out in their closets, things they use daily. I wrote a bunch of songs while toiling away at Dependable. Although this song doesn't have a deep meaning to anybody else, it means plenty to me.

The cooler is the part of you that has fun and mingles with all your friends. It makes people happy. You pack it full of ice and alcohol and everybody smiles when they open it up. The skateboard represents the part of you that you've tucked away for too long and when you finally reveal it to everybody, you're awkward and rusty. It's better to always be yourself, all the time. Perhaps I'm just trying to make sense of a song written while drunk. I was young....... Don't judge.

Cooler has never been seen until now. Through all the years of the Posse, this is the first the first time I've let anybody read or hear the lyrics. This song has never been played in public......for obvious reasons.

COOLER

Cooler,
Comin' out of the closet to keep all my drinks cold
Until it gets too warm and then the ice just melts away.
Cooler,
I take you back inside and fill you up with ice
Then we go back outside and drink more cold beer on the porch.
Cooler,
You've been kind and when the weather is fine
I take you to the park where complete strangers open you up.

Coolers are good for the summer time world (3X)
Coolers are good to me

Skateboard,
We've been apart too long, just let me hit this bong
Then we will go outside and I will ride you on Scott's big ramp
Skateboard,
I've gained 40 pounds and I'm looking kinda round
But we'll still go to the top of this ramp and ride it down
Skateboard,
I'm way up in the air, I don't see you anywhere
Now I have fallen down real hard and broken both of my thumbs

Skateboards are fun if you know how to ride (3X)
Skateboards are bad for me

GUNFIGHT CREW

This is the verse and hook I wrote for a song that the great Frank Boss and I had worked on. We had made a couple rap songs through the years and had started to write some new tracks. We planned on rebranding ourselves as "The Gunfight Crew". I think there is a rough recording of this hiding somewhere.

GUNFIGHT CREW

Ah yes, it's the gunfight crew (2X)

Here we go, nice and slow
Get your body on the floor
It's the Gunfight Crew and we be knocking at your door
Lookin' for something a little fun
Or maybe something to sip.
We hoping the party just hasn't begun
Take you on a lyric trip too...

The place where it all began,
Like the son of Sam, or Jake and the fat man (not really)
Here it is, this is our master plan
It ain't no pyramid scam, Like Anthrax said "Yo I'm the man"
Let's keep it popping, we can go all night
So shake your hips to the right
We'll have you feeling pure delight, outta sight
You can't see me, we in the place you wanna be
It's not a tree, I don't watch Glee
I like to study history
So here we go…

Ah yes, it's the gunfight crew (2X)

FRONT DOOR

This is yet another song I wrote about a hard relationship. Are you catching onto the theme of my writing? Both parts, the girl and the guy, represented how I was feeling at the time. I wanted to leave because I was over all the drama and infidelities, yet I also wanted everything to work out because it meant that much to me. I still believed in the thought of "us". But as we all learn in life, it takes two committed people to make a relationship work.

FRONT DOOR

She grabbed her coat
Made her way to the front door
She left a note
"I can't do this anymore"
 You know we tried so hard to make this right
When it's good it's great, but damn I really hate these fights
Can I really spend my life like this?
If dreams come true than this will be my final wish"

May the laughter never stop, may we climb up to the top
Looking down upon our happy life
May I be the air you breathe? Can I tell you everything?
I just want to believe in you

Alone in bed
Tossing, thinking about the words that she wrote
The things he said
Never meant to be the old hangman's rope
Now he smokes his last cigarette
Burns it to the filter feels the shame and his regrets
Can he really spend his life like this?
If dreams come true than this would be his final wish

May the laughter never stop, may we climb up to the top
And look down at all the happy times
May I be the air you breathe? can I tell you everything?
I just want to believe in you

Things have changed but did love really ever fade away?
Could one kiss release the passion and relieve the pain
If there's one left to say or do
Please remember, (that)I love you

May the laughter never stop, may we climb up to the top
And look down at all the happy times
May I be the air you breathe; can I tell you everything
I just want to believe in you

CASHED OUT

This is a fast-little song about when you get those feelings that your relationship is solely based upon your bank account and not the immeasurable things you offer somebody else like love, time, respect; all the things that mean everything until they are gone. Sometimes it's best just to settle your tab and get out while you can.

CASHED OUT

Hey pretty baby tell me, why do you act this way?
Is our love only based upon the money that I make?
You said you loved it when I'd look deep into your eyes.
Now it seems you only want me if my wallets supersized!

Hey pretty baby I loved you from your head down to your toes
Are we gonna be together why only heaven knows.
You should have told me that money was your best friend.
Now you see this game is over and I'm cashing my chips in!

I'm working day and night, I work my fingers to the bone
Girl you got me feeling like this house just ain't my home
Will you ever be happy? Will you ever be content?
Am I really here for you or do I only pay your rent?

Hey pretty baby I loved you from your head down to your toes
Are we gonna be together why only heaven knows.
You should have told me that money was your best friend.
Now you see this game is over and I'm cashing my chips in!

Ohhh…. I'm cashing my chips in. (4x)

ON THE SHELF

This is another track dealing with people in our life who always judge you and tell you how to be, yet they are falling apart. Some people feel it is necessary to minimalize others in order to feel superior, but in the end, it all catches up with them. A wise man once said, "Wherever you go, there you are". You can't run from yourself and hurting others to feel better accomplishes nothing.

On The Shelf

Some say that life is rough, but for the life you live you ain't
tough enough, you go and
Blame everybody for the life that you live
You only take, never give
You a grown-up or you a kid?
Keep on expressing all your hopes and your fears
Through all the smiles and the tears
You look back, see wasted years
Never knowing where you are headed next, Is it a gate or a fence
I said, "come on just take a rest"
Say that them people try to hold you down
 You're a queen with no crown
 But you act like a clown, and...
You isolate yourself from all of the rest
Ya you say you're the best, but c'mon you failed the test.
I kept believing in your mirrors and smoke
You say, "it's only a joke"
But I feel like I'm choking
You never ever did believe in yourself
All that you care for is wealth
I put you back on the shelf cuz….

You don't understand me.
If the feeling was right you might, comprehend me

Talking all about how the feelings were wrong
That's why I wrote you this song
Why did you string me along?
I gave you everything that one man could give
Became a dad for your kid
You were my reason to live, But…
It can never fill up all the empty inside
You priced your soul and your pride
That's when the perfect you died

I must confess that though I tried to believe
Broke my heart made it bleed
Now I'm drowned in your sea

Patrick Rodgers

I thought that I could always call you my friend
 My true love companion, my best friend to the end
Came up upon another fork in the road
Which one will lead me home, I'm carrying a heavy load
Of doubt, regrets, remorse, compassion and pain
But man it all feels the same
Like I've been hit by your train cuz

You don't understand me
If the feeling was right, you might, comprehend me

THE BACON SONG

I was walking on the beach on day with a friend and we were talking about the current state of music. Modern rap and hip-hop sucks (in my opinion). I expressed that most of the lyrics being written today are meaningless and most of it is disposable. "I could write a song about bacon and if the bass hit right it will be a hit". I never recorded a rap version but I think you can find the stripped down acoustic one on YouTube if you look hard enough.

The Bacon Song

She got the bacon bacon (2X)
Like when it's in the pan you see it moving, popping, shaking
She got the bacon bacon (2X)
I ate so damn much that it left my whole-body aching

She got the pan so hot I couldn't touch it with my hand
She lays them out so nice they sizzled like hot skin on sand
Shit started popping I said girl you better just beware
Maybe use a splatter screen don't wanna get it in your hair
The house was smelling fine the scent had taken over me
About to lose control I said don't make me wait baby She said
Hold on a minute I'm gonna slowly count to three
And when I'm done you know this bacons gonna be crispy

She got the bacon bacon (2X)
Like when it's in the pan you see it moving, popping, shaking
She got the bacon bacon (2X)
I ate so damn much that it left my whole-body aching

Could you put it on some bread
With lettuce, tomato, mayo please?
Or maybe by some eggs, I'd like them to be cooked over easy
Put it on some salad girl, just crush them up all itty bitty
You're driving me crazy baby, you got me begging on my knees

She got the bacon bacon (2X)
Like when it's in the pan you see it moving, popping, shaking
She got the bacon bacon (2X)
I ate so damn much that it left my whole-body aching

BOOM (GOOD DAY TO DIE)

I was reading the newspaper one day when I stumbled upon an article about the homeless veteran population. At the time, I believe it was almost 40,000 veterans were homeless on any given night. Although I may not agree with some military actions, I do believe it is the duty of our government to take care of those that follow the orders and put their lives on the line. I don't know how one can put others life in danger for what they feel is a justifiable cause, only do discard them when they return home.

If you want to help, look up your local homeless veteran organization. Many of the national organizations spend too much money on payroll and advertising. Find a local charity that helps homeless veterans and help your community.

Boom (Good Day to Die)

When I'm sitting out on the streets
You pretend that you can't see me
Your lazy eyes make you look so blind
But I don't think I can find the time
To sit and listen to how you cry
About the way that the world was mine
Tell me that I have to leave
Cause you say that you can't stand me

Boom Boom Boom goes the shots to the sky
What a day, day, day, day, what a good day to die

Send me over to a foreign land
With no clear mission, and no exit plan
When I come back, you don't care about me
Only money, for your friends and colleagues
Body is broken got PTSD
But I ain't asking for your sympathy
Have you listened to a word I've said?
Sometimes I wonder if I'm better off dead

Boom Boom Boom goes the shots to the sky
What a day, day, day, day, what a good day to die

SHOOT THE SHOOTER

Shoot the Shooter was written about Brad Will, a photojournalist that was shot dead while filming the teachers strike in Oaxaca, Mexico. He was targeted by the local government for his willingness to shed light upon the atrocities happening in the region. In his final video, voices are heard demanding that he stops filming. As he is being scolded for continuing to film, a gunshot is heard and Brad Will lets out a scream. The camera drops to the ground. Brad Will later died from two gunshot wounds. 4 local officials were held responsible for his murder. For more information Google/YouTube search: Brad Will Oaxaca

Shoot the Shooter

Went down south just to see if he
Could find the truth with the camera's eye
Bones are broken, them wounds start to bleed
Radio screams out a warning, but the language he does not speak
Felt the bullet fell down to his knee

(Shoot the shooter)
Kill the one with cameras what the radio says
(Shoot the shooter)
Put one in his chest and two more in his head
(Shoot the shooter)
Will is a weapon of equality
Little did he know that his murder, would be his legacy

See the red shirts they coming
Flanked on both sides by the white
Looks like their angry at teachers
Trying to teach the children what's right
Hand in line with their shoulders
See the brilliant flash of the light
Camera catches the last frame
Five people lost their lives, THEIR LIVES!

(Shoot the shooter)
Kill the one with cameras what the radio says
(Shoot the shooter)
Put one in his chest and two more in his head
(Shoot the shooter)
Will is a weapon of equality
Little did he know that his murder, would be his legacy

HEADLINES

As I've grown older and had the privilege of growing up during the arrival of cable tv and the 24-hour news networks; I have witnessed the power of suggestion that television has on the population. Since my daughter was born, have become even more aware of the influence television has on the youth of today (as well as everybody else that watches). The opening lines represent the beginning of a newscast where they throw out one-liners to draw you in to watching, casually putting the weather right next to a story of a deceased stripper, a traffic report next to a bank robbery. The second verse addresses how the news can be skewed to highlight certain people or positions, often ignoring all sides to a story and how the programs influence the nation. I feel we need less tv and more conversations in this world

Headlines

A drunken stripper found dead in a hotel room
A high of 90^0
Maybe some light showers at noon
Traffics backed up on 19 again.
A middle aged white man robs a bank so he can eat
He's got a family, been kicked out on the street
He got a handgun, Drove a minivan for a getaway car

Do you watch T.V.?
Is it real or fantasy?
They tell one sided stories make us think what they believe
Must see T.V.
Fox News or NBC
Truth is stranger than fiction in this world of lust and greed
I don't believe it, oh but I see it
It's on T.V.

Some crooked politicians in the spotlight center stage
They throw em softballs, But just right out of camera range
A man of the people is ignored again
A hack no talent heiress fills the prime time tv screen
Her bad example, is there, for everyone to see
She's making millions, She's number 1 with all the tweens

Do you watch T.V.?
Is it real or fantasy?
They tell one sided stories make us think what they believe
Must see T.V.
Fox News or NBC
Truth is stranger than fiction in this world of lust and greed
I don't believe it, oh but I see it
It's on T.V.

The revolution, is near
And let me make this clear
We're not gonna follow, fake plastic trends
Yes, I'll be me, I'm free until the end
We won't break or bend.

B & B

Just a little poem I wrote.

B & B

From Botox to Boob Jobs
Sun-In to spray tans
The only thing real about you, is the way you use a man
You sell him on things, like your goals and your plans
But they're all just pipe dreams, shady schemes and a sham
All of the things that you say are a lie
"I love you. I want you. I need you" …. Goodbye
You sucked them all in with your tales of forever
Roll out of bed, look at them, say "Whatever"
Blame them for your failure, never look at yourself
Trade your family for money, all you care for is wealth
You said your laid back, you just go with the flow
But it's on your back you lay, you're a dirt bag, a ho.
You say that you've changed, yet you're always the same
Now your old and alone, and you're the only one to blame.

And In The End…

So there you have it. Some of the first and last songs I ever wrote. Many of these songs worked in both the punk rock and country categories. I never really cared what style they were played in, I just wanted someone to listen. I guess that's all any musician wants, someone to listen to what they have to say. I always wanted to be able to write a happy, pop song. For some strange reason I only seemed to be inspired by the tragic relationships I threw myself into. Perhaps I felt creativity only came through pain, perhaps I enjoyed the suffering. Who knows?

Some 20 years after I wrote my first song, I still find myself drawn to songs of struggle and strife, songs of those in bad relationships and those of hopeless romantics. Songs I wish I had written and those I wish I couldn't relate too, but I do. They say misery loves company, and I'm always looking for a few friends.

Printed in Great Britain
by Amazon

85634231R00031